STICK COMBATIVES

THE KENGLA MILITARY METHOD

STICK COMBATIVES

The Kengla Military Method

STICK COMBATIVES

THE KENGLA MILITARY METHOD

TWIN RAVENS

PUBLISHING

Edited by

Fernan Vargas and James Loriega

First Printing: January 2020

ISBN: 978-1-79485-709-4

Twin Ravens Publishing
Chicago, Illinois USA 60107

TWIN RAVENS PUBLISHING

DEDICATION

Col William A. Kengla, USMC,
(6/25/1910 – 1/3/1993)

This volume is dedicated to the memory of **William A. Kengla** *and the other unsung pioneers of Military Combatives whose names and contributions have been forgotten as we ignorantly practice and pass on the teachings they left us.*

Disclaimer Notice

STICK COMBATIVES

THE KENGLA MILITARY METHOD

Contents

Authors' Caveat

This book is primarily intended for the purposes of entertainment and information, and not meant to be used as a training guide without the guidance of a qualified instructor. Readers interested in using the book as a training guide should contact Fernan Vargas, who can put you in contact with a qualified instructor to guide you or assist you himself.

PREFACE

The name *Bruce Lee* is recognizable by most people around to world, whether the person hearing it is a *Jeet Kune Do* practitioner, a *Wing Chun* exponent, trains in a different martial art, or can't punch his way out of a paper bag. If pressed to explain why Mr. Lee's name is so well-recognized, most will answer that his fame is deserved for his vast accomplishments in the martials arts.

Perhaps … but ironically, only *one-tenth* of the same population will be familiar with the name *Jun-Fan Li*. The remaining ninety percent will plead ignorance of the name and admit to being oblivious to that person's accomplishments. Of course you, the reader, know that these two names belong to same man.

Jun-Fan Li vs. Bruce Lee

So, *what is the point here?*

Our objective here is to make two obvious but unfortunate points—

   1) fame and notoriety are fickle and arbitrary and, as a result

   2) there exist many individuals whose names and accomplishments are not duly recognized.

As far back as 1647, Baltasar Gracian, SJ, the most astute observer of his fellow Man, wrote—

> *Fortune* and *Fame*: Where the one is fickle the other is enduring. The first for life, the second afterwards; the one against envy, the other against oblivion. Fortune is desired, at times assisted: fame is earned. The desire for fame springs from man's best part. It was and is the sister of the Giants; it always goes to extremes—either horrible monsters or brilliant prodigies.

If you are familiar with this sharp-minded Jesuit philosopher, you're clearly a well-read martial artist; if not, that's fine—and you have proven my point:*there exist many individuals whose names and accomplishments have not been recognized.*

Another such person—and the one directly related to this book—was **William Archibald Kengla.** *Who*, you might ask, *was William Archibald Kengla?* Read on.

Part I

Preliminaries

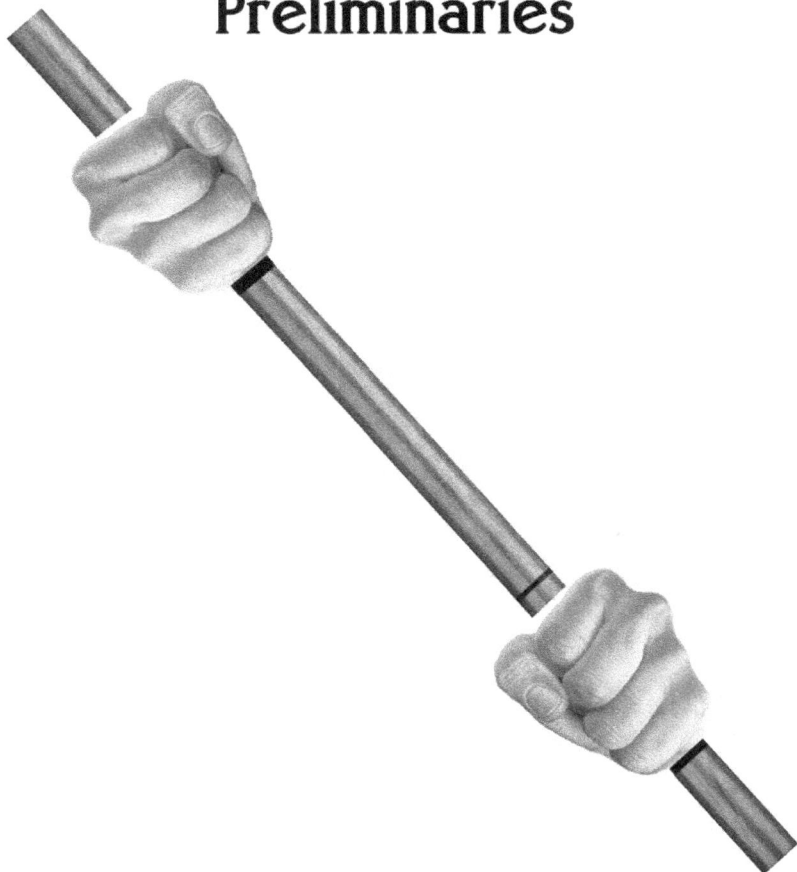

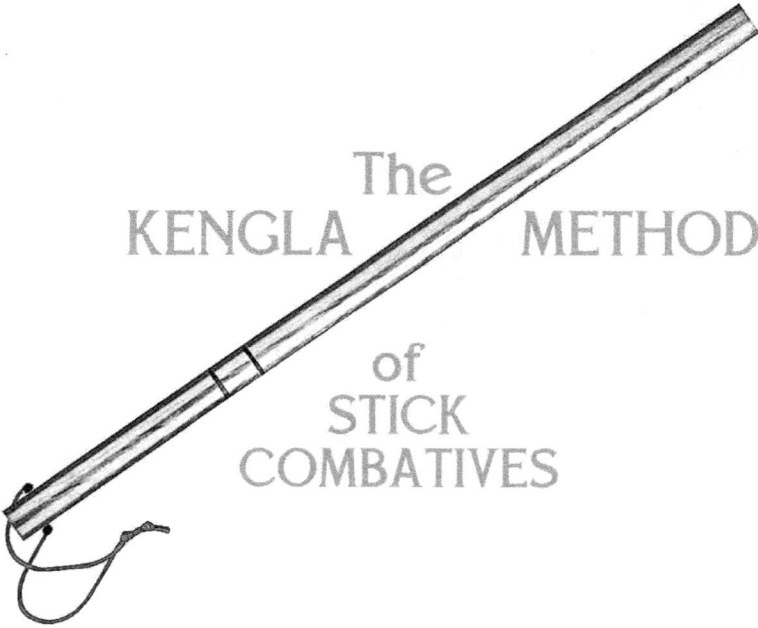

The
KENGLA METHOD
of
STICK
COMBATIVES

INTRODUCTION

I received my first copy of John Styers's book, **Cold Steel,** as a Christmas gift in 1996. This was the first time I encountered the name *William Kengla*. The name stuck with me in the back of my head. I suppose that if his name had been Smith, it would not have; but Kengla was a unique name and as it turns out he was also a unique man.

Kengla was a decorated Colonel in the United States Marine Corp, author, and professor. Like John Styers, Kengla had been a pupil of A. J. Biddle, and studied individual combat at the United States Marine Corp Basic School for Officers. After that, Kengla continued his working relationship with Biddle and is attributed with having created many of the attack and defense sequences included in Biddle's classic work, **Do or Die.**

Styers also recognized the value in the work of Col. Kengla. Kengla's influence on Modern Combatives appears again in Styers' book, **Cold Steel**. Styers, in fact, credits Kengla as the originator of the *stick method* presented in **Cold Steel.**

I have always been something of a contrarian by nature and the method presented was of great interest to me. The prospect of an effective stick method that was not based on the ever-popular Filipino martial arts was a very attractive idea. While the Filipino arts have much to offer, they have inadvertently contributed to the groupthink mentality of instructors in the field. Many instructors have lost sight of the fact that there are many time- and battle-tested methods in the historical record, including methods more suitable and relevant to the needs of the modern Combatives practitioner.

I have worked this stick method for many years, with many training partners, and it remains a part of my Combatives curriculum. Yet, omewhat surprisingly, I have found few instructors who have adopted this method, and even fewer who even knew who Kengla was.

While Kengla's contemporaries—e.g., *Styers, Biddle, Fairbairn,* and *Applegate*—have all carved out their well-deserved niches in military and martial history, Kengla remains an unsung hero in the realm of WWII-era Combatives. For me, and for Mr. Loriega, this book is an attempt to rectify this situation by casting a spotlight on a man who is duly deserving of recognition for his contributions to the field.

—Fernan Vargas

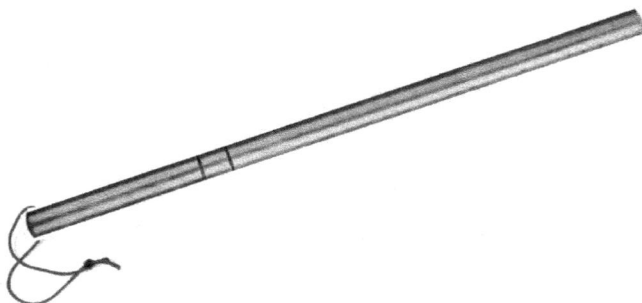

MILITARY STICK COMBAT

The word *military* invariably conjures up images of marching troops, tanks running roughshod over the main streets of a captured city, or anti-aircraft guns attempting to bring down enemy fighter planes. Military is synonymous with *modern*, *massive*, and *mechanized*—and *hardly* the words one associates with the *stick* as a weapon. Even the notion of a "military stick" is as incongruous as that of a "pacifist's knuckle-duster." And yet, we know that the stick has had a formal place in modern military training since the start of the 20th century—side by side with the pistol, rifle, and hand-thrown grenade.

The chronological history of the military stick use in the modern age would include all the best-known hand-to-hand combat instructors, including—

- A. J. Biddle
- Eric A. Sykes
- William E. Fairbairn
- Rex Applegate, and
- Michael Echani.

Each of these men was a major influencers, if not framers, of military training policy, not just a friendly neighborhood arnis instructor, giving pointers to LEOs at the local precinct. The stick's significance for the military is thus reflected in each of their training curricula, as well as in the books these men wrote and left as their legacy.

And those are just the names you recognize. There were many others, like Col Kengla, whose contributions to Combatives in general, and the stick in particular, have been as significant as they are unnoticed...

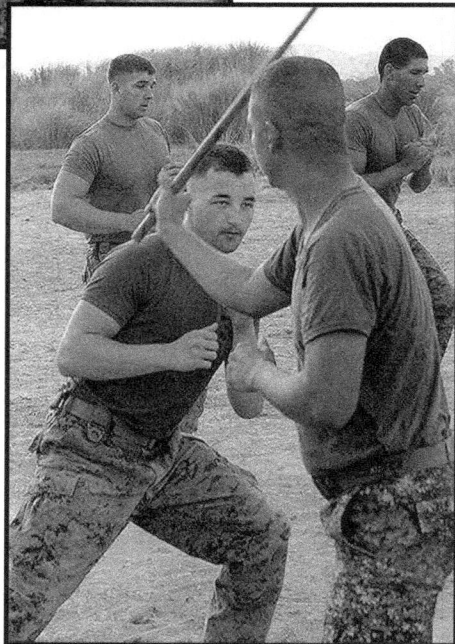

Modern-day Marines training in Stick Combatives

THE KENGLA MILITARY METHOD

Like all Military Combatives systems, Kengla's method is simple and logical. The material as presented in **Cold Steel** is completely serviceable. To be clear, the method is not a comprehensive stick-based martial art, such as Filipino *kali* or Japanese *hanbojutsu*—it is a method meant to be taught, learned, and completed in a short period of time. The method provides the student with ***survival essentials***; that is, a minimum effective proficiency for self-protection.

This must not be interpeted to mean that the method is lacking in substance. In fact, the method is *fully* functional and can be as advanced as the student wishes to make it. After all, *advanced* material is merely the result of *basics performed well*.

Properly drilled and trained over time, this method provides the diligent pratitioner with a highly effective and reliable skillset in the use of the stick. Kengla's method is intuitive and can stand alone or serve as a source for rich extrapolation.

Origins

The origin of the material, however, is less known than its effectiveness. Although the Kengla material has been shared with practitioners of Japanese *bojutsu* as well as with instructors in police and military baton methods, there is no consensus as to its genesis.

**British Bobby
with Truncheon**

**Truncheon
with Sheath**

Koryu Bugei Impact Weapons

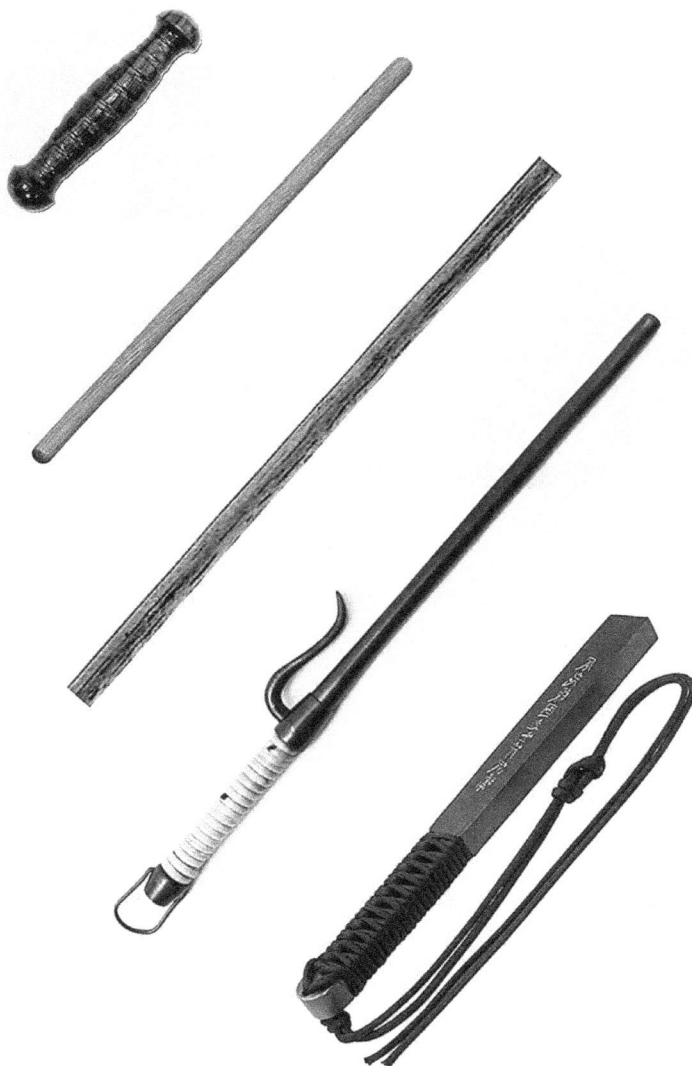

From top, down: **Tenouchi** ("Yawara stick"); **Hishigi; Tanbo; Jutte; Tessen**.
(*Courtesy, New York Ninpokai collection*)

In some instances, the Kengla techniques resemble both Japanese *tanbojutsu* and turn-of-the-century *truncheon* of the British bobby. Both are potentially plausible sources.

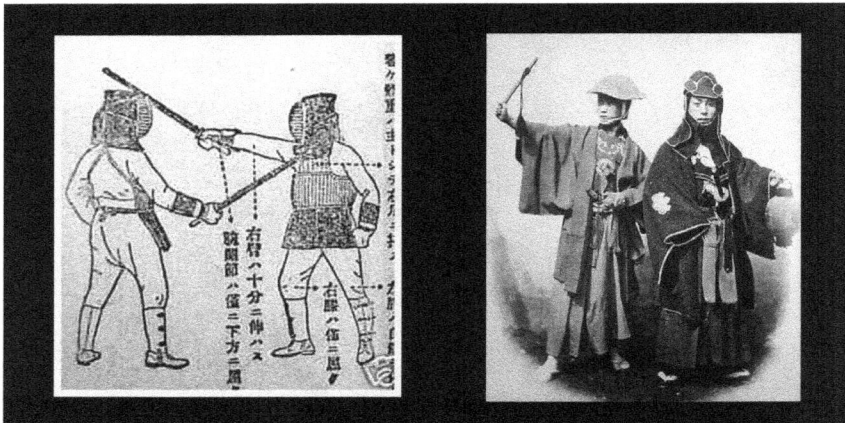

19th Century images: Tanbo training; Samurai patrol with *tanbo* and *lantern*

William Fairbairn, the founder of *Defendu*, drew heavily from both eastern and western fighting arts when creating his system, as did William Barton-Wright before him, and many others after. This juxtaposition and blending of techniques from disparate sources was, in fact, a common practice for instructors of their era.

We know that Kengla spent time in Shanghai. *Is it likely that he and Fairbairn crossed paths?* If they did, the record of such a meeting is lost to time, but that does not change the probability that Kengla was exposed to various methods. Regardless of where the material comes from, it works! And when it comes to Military Combatives, that is the *only* litmus test that matters.

Part II

Fundamentals

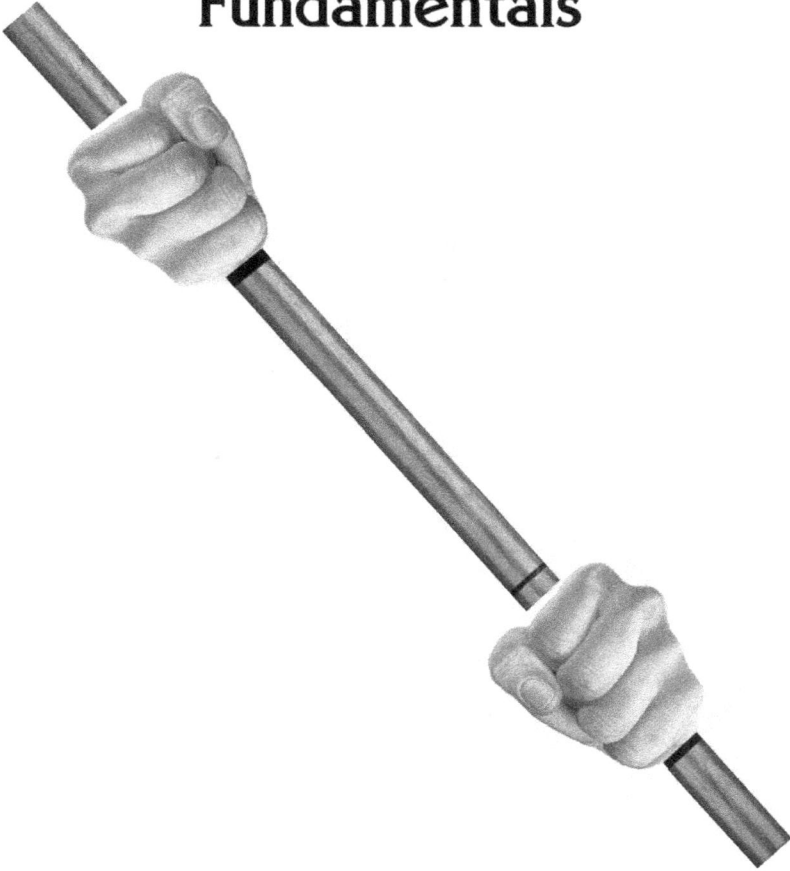

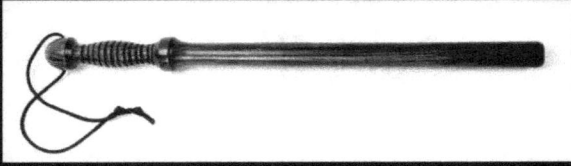

Biddle   **Fairbairn**

Applegate   **Echanis**

Pioneers of the
Military Stick

STICK NOMENCLATURE

In order to discuss the nature of the stick as a field expedient weapon, it is necessary to establish working definitions related to its parts. The original nomenclature terms for the Military Stick are derived from the policeman's and MP's nightstick. The difference, however, is that on the nightstick these terms are fixed, while on the Military Stick the terms for its parts are fluid. This is because whichever end of the stick one grabs becomes the *grip* (with pommel), with the distal end becoming the *tip*.

The Tip

The tip of the baton is usually small and rounded, about the size of a small marble. Larger designs are available which can be as large as a large ball bearing.

The Shaft

The shaft is the area of the stick that runs from tip to pommel.

The Grip

The grip begins one to two inches above the pommel. The grip is the primary area from which the stick is held.

The Pommel

The pommel is the bottom of the stick just bellow the grip. The pommel is a used as a striking surface for extremely close quarters.

Military Stick
Nomenclature

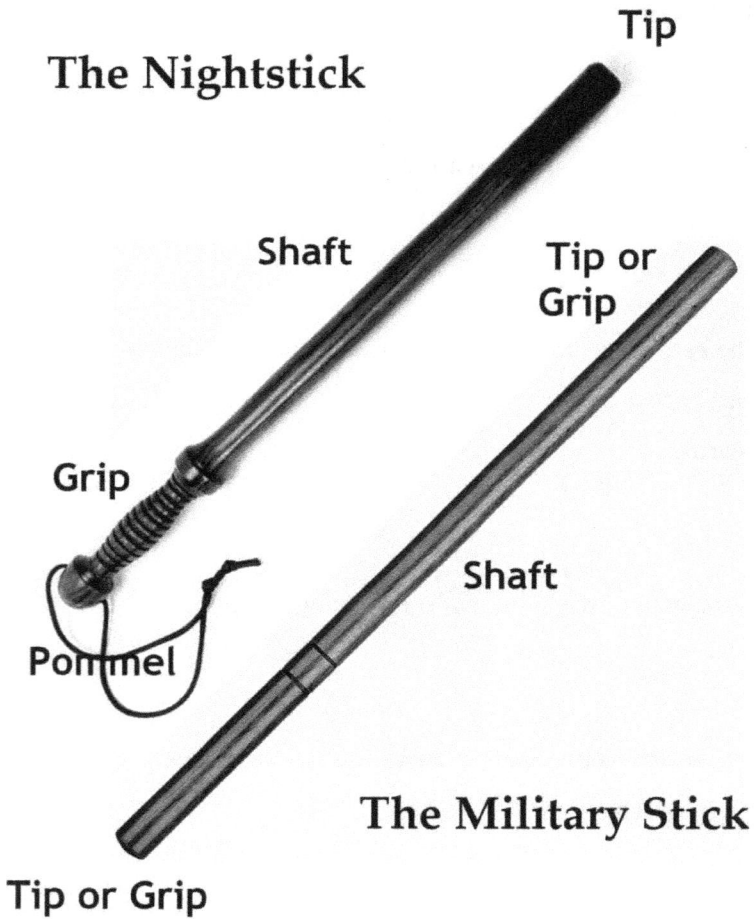

Tip

The Nightstick

Shaft

Tip or
Grip

Grip

Shaft

Pommel

The Military Stick

Tip or Grip

GRIPS

The Short End Grip

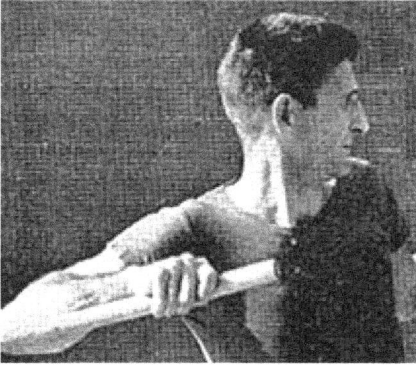

Grab it just as you would a KNIFE. The fingers are wrapped securely around it, allowing approximately three inches of the stick to protrude OUT IN FRONT of your hand. The remainder of the stick lies along the forearm, forming a straight line from the point to the elbow. Now allow the long end of the stick to drop by your side.

The short end technique. Grasp your stick about three inches below the forward end; the body must be very well balanced.

The Short End Bar Grip

This grip is executed by whipping the stick to the left and into your left hand with a simple wrist movement. You will now have your left-hand palm down and your right-hand palm up.

The Long End Grip

Grasp the stick a few inches from the BACK. This protrusion is a *reserve* for clubbing in close or smashing back at an opponent who may attack you from the rear. The LONG END of the stick is out in front - held out like a knife. The point and the elbow form a STRAIGHT LINE.

The Long End Bar Grip

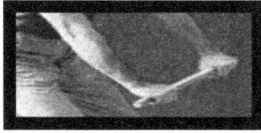

The stick is readily converted to the bar position by flicking long end over to the other hand with a simple wrist movement. In attacks, from the *long end technique*, a bar may also be formed with a movement of the RIGHT WRIST. Unlike the Right-hand grasp used in the *short end technique* where the RIGHT KNUCKLES are DOWN - the fingers UP - the bar formed from the long end stance will have the knuckles on BOTH hands UP.

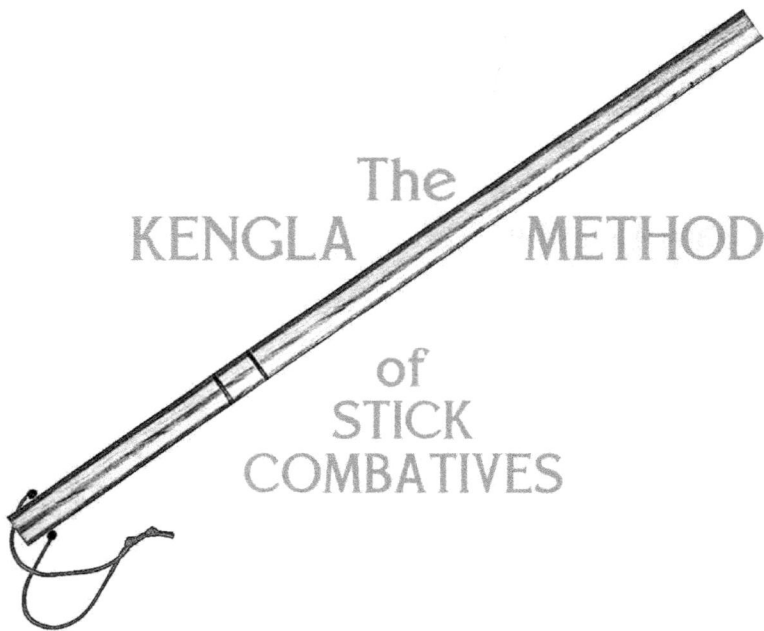

The
KENGLA METHOD
of
STICK
COMBATIVES

THE STANCE

Knife-Fighter's Stance　　　　**Boxer's Stance**

Your stance may be either that of the knife fighter (*right* foot forward) or that of the boxer (*left* foot forward). However, the left foot forward, stick in the right hand, is recommended for most situations.

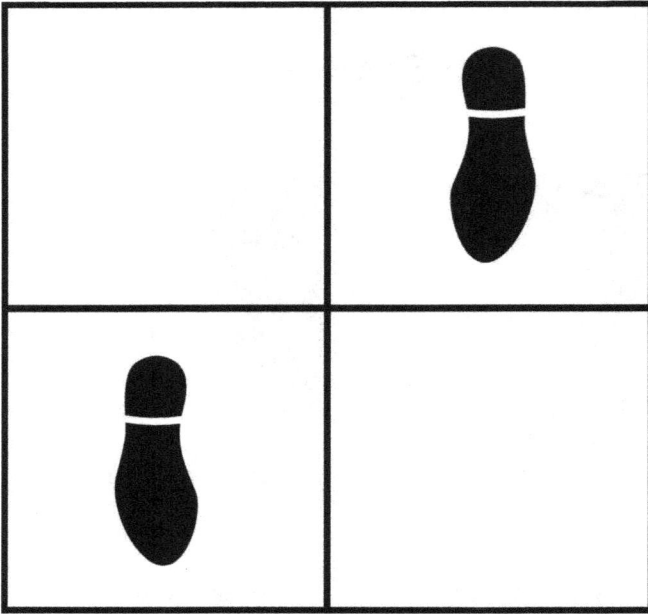

Knife-fighter's Stance

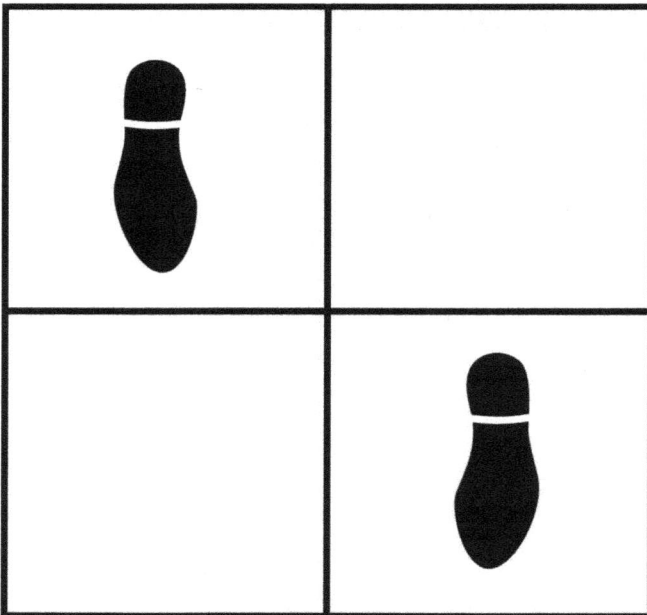

Boxer's Stance

OFFENSIVE MOVEMENTS

The Attack

ANY ONE of the blows described here will be decisive if planted properly in a vital target area. Your choice of attack will depend upon the situation.

The Long End Technique

Fundamentally, this technique is the use of the stick in the same way you would use a knife. In combat, if you are otherwise unarmed, find a club and sharpen both ends with a rock. Since you have no cutting edge, direct the whipping action of the club to your opponent's temple, neck. shoulders, joints and muscles. Use the point in full thrusts.

The Long End Thrust

Thrust the point of the stick into your enemy's solar plexus. Your left arm whips back, adding power and velocity to blow.

The Long End Slash

Slash with the long end of your stick in the same manner in which a sabre is used, striking at enemy's joints and muscles.

The Long End Bar Whip Strike

The stick is readily converted to the bar position by flicking long end over to the other hand with a simple wrist movement. When you assume this position with your bar, you are in an effective nonaggressive stance, but bar is ready for action. The bar may be used to smash or the stick may be whipped from either end by releasing the grasp of either hand.

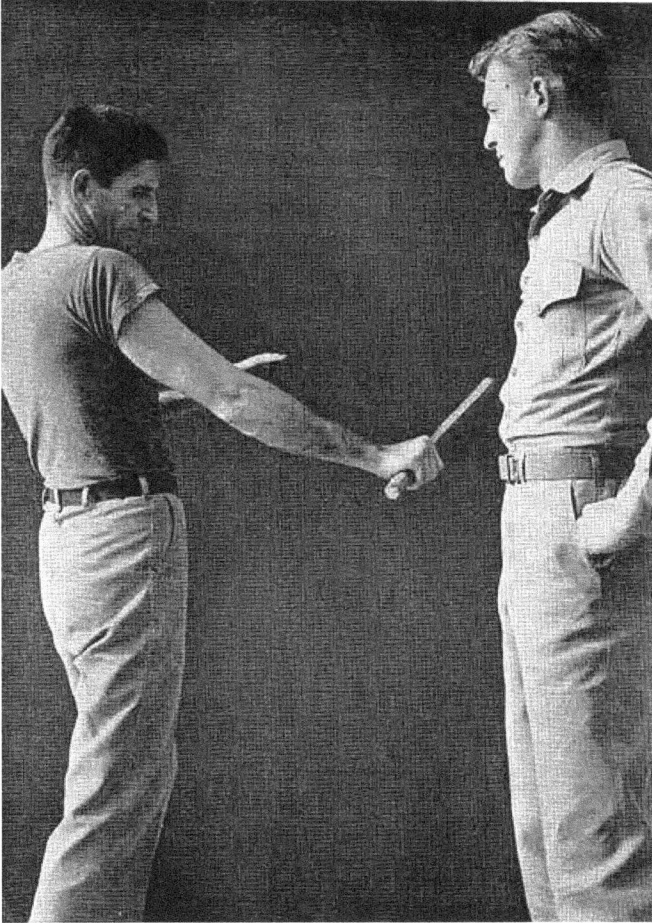

To strike for an exposed target on the opponent's right side, release the grip of your left hand and strike with your right.

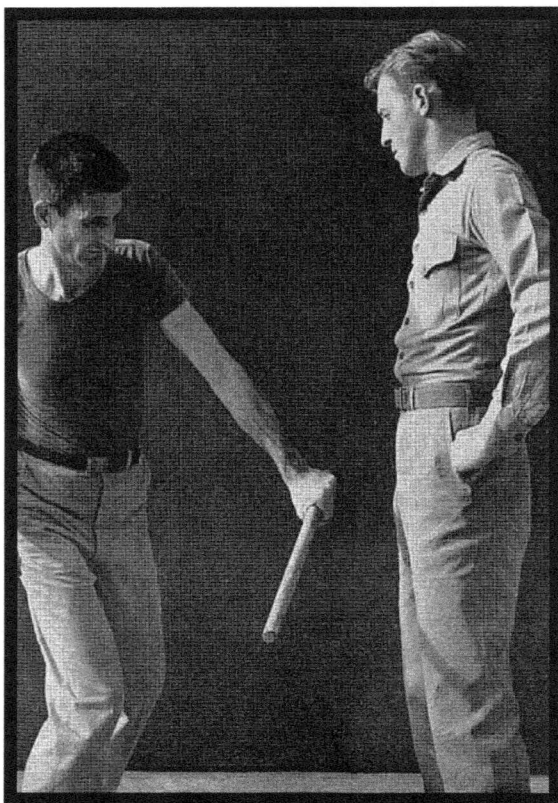

To strike at a target on the opponent's left side, release the right hand and smash across, holding your stick with the left.

The Solar Plexus Blow

The Solar plexus blow is delivered from the boxer's stance, your stick cocked against your forearm, your LEFT foot forward. With a driving, piston-like action of the stick arm, you smash the stick directly into the solar plexus of your opponent. The blow is carried in with additional force by advancing the right foot as you strike. If you CONNECTED, you have succeeded in discouraging your opponent and he will show no more interest in the fight.

Your stick performs a piston-like motion as it is whipped up along the forearm and thrust into exposed target.

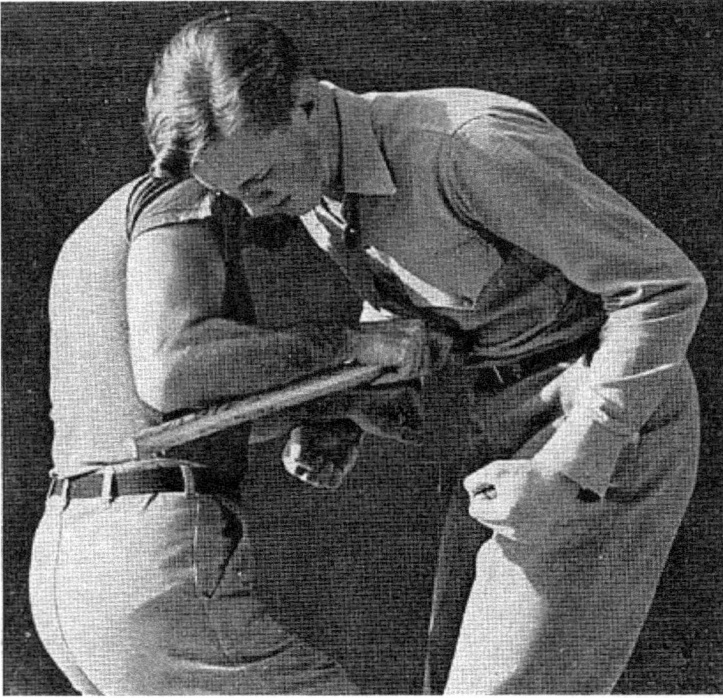

The opponent's solar plexus is your target. The impact is on end of your stick, backed by power of full arm and shoulder.

The Upward Smash

Your stick will form a bar in a split second if you whip it to the left and into your left hand with a simple wrist movement.

If you missed or if your blow was blocked, FOLLOW THROUGH by WHIPPING the LONG END of the stick over to your left side with a single movement of the WRIST. Your LEFT HAND, PALM DOWN, should be ready to receive. Your stick is now a HORIZONTAL BAR, gripped in both hands and held at a midsection level.

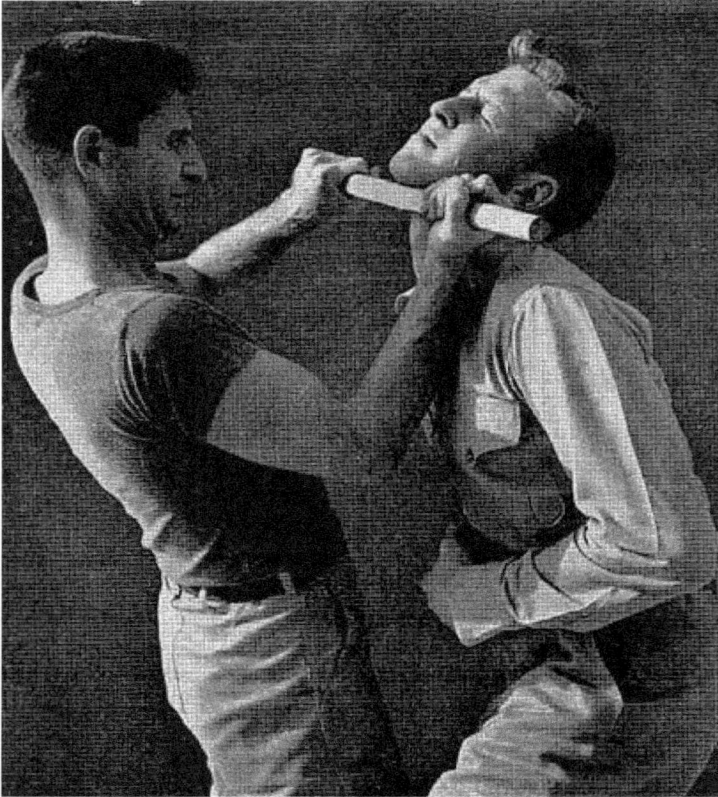

The bar is smashed up under chin with the full power of the arms and shoulders. Complete smash with full follow through. DRIVE the bar up UNDER THE CHIN of your opponent.

The Downward Smash

All right, so you missed on the way up-SMASH IT ACROSS THE BRIDGE of his nose ON THE WAY D0WN. Draw it back to yourself and smash it straight to his nose, teeth or throat. If your opponent is still obstinate, MOVE IN.

If you missed or merely grazed the chin, leaving bar over opponent's head, you are in a position to continue the attack.

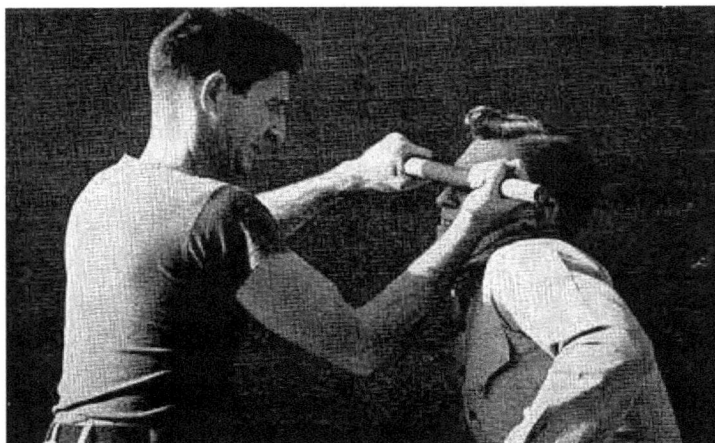

Follow through with a sweeping downward smash. Bring the bar crashing down on enemy's nose if his face is turned up.

The Direct Smash

Bring bar back, close to chest, and prepare for direct smash.

Bar is smashed into enemy's throat, or head between the eyes.

The Short End Thrust

Grab enemy's shirt and return your stick to forearm position.

To MOVE IN, release the left side of the stick and bring it back, along the forearm, into its original position. Now, with your FREE LEFT HAND GRAB A SOLID HUNK OF YOUR OPPONENT'S CLOTHING, somewhere around his right shoulder area and pull him in close. *From now on, wherever he goes, you go!* Start smashing with the SHORT END of the stick - duck low and drive it into his groin, solar plexus or rib area. Strike ANYWHERE, let him have it under the chin if you can get there with it.

Crouch low; smash the small end of stick up to enemy's groin.

If the groin attack misses, try for your enemy's solar plexus.

If you are attacked from the rear while engaging an enemy, drive the long end of your stick straight back at the offender.

Direct short end of stick to opponent's neck, jaw or temple. Anywhere the weapon lands will be a painfully damaged spot.

If he is blocking your targets, start swinging around the OUTSIDE. Try for his temple, ear, jaw or side of the neck; try for a blow in his lower rib section. ANYWHERE your point lands will be a painfully damaged spot. And a lot of sore spots add up to ONE BIG PAIN. And a painfully bruised body offers LESS RESISTANCE.

The Pivot Punch

Now, you may wish to resort to a PIVOT PUNCH. This outlawed boxing blow is delivered like a right hook to the opponent's jaw, but the point of the elbow, rather than the fist, contacts the target. The upper arm, shoulder to elbow, is too short to deliver this blow effectively without accompanying the blow with a *wheeling body movement*.

The stick is kept along the arm, protecting your elbow as it smashes across your opponent's head after your *right hook swing*. When you deliver this blow, put plenty of "WHEELING BODY" behind it DON'T PULL YOUR PUNCH!

For the pivot punch, bring the long end of the stick securely along the forearm. Stick will protect your elbow as it strikes.

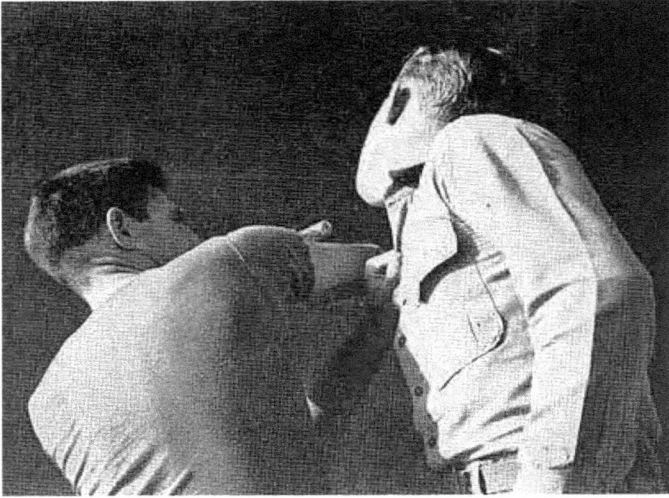

Pivot the body and apply a right elbow smash to enemy's jaw.

DEFENSIVE MOVEMENTS

To Block A Kick

To block a kick, whip the long end of the stick across to your left hand. It has again become a horizontal bar, but instead of bringing it up to his chin, snap the arms straight down at the oncoming leg. Aim for the shinbone if possible; then follow up with a chin smash since the stick is in a position for this movement.

If your opponent attempts to kick, snap your stick over into the bar position. Your feet firmly placed; body well balanced.

Snap your arms straight, directing your bar to the shin of opponent's raised leg; lock arms against power of his kick.

To Block An Overhead Attack

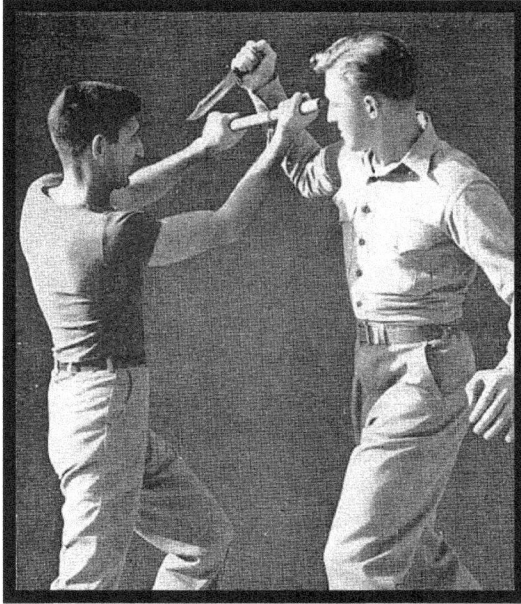

Smash your arms out straight against a down swinging blow. Make use of your feet or knees against any exposed target.

Your opponent's overhand or underhand blows may be blocked in this same manner. Smash straight out for the descending arm, or bash aside the upcoming arm. FOLLOW THROUGH AT ANY TARGET OPENING.

To Block An Underhand Attack

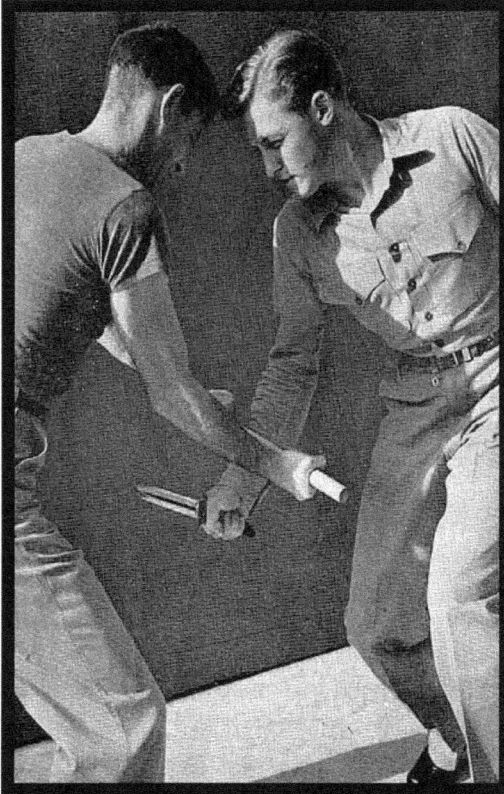

If your opponent tries an up-swinging blow, direct your bar straight for his wrist or forearm. Draw trunk out of range.

At the completion of any block with your bar, follow through immediately with a smash to enemy's forehead, chin, or throat.

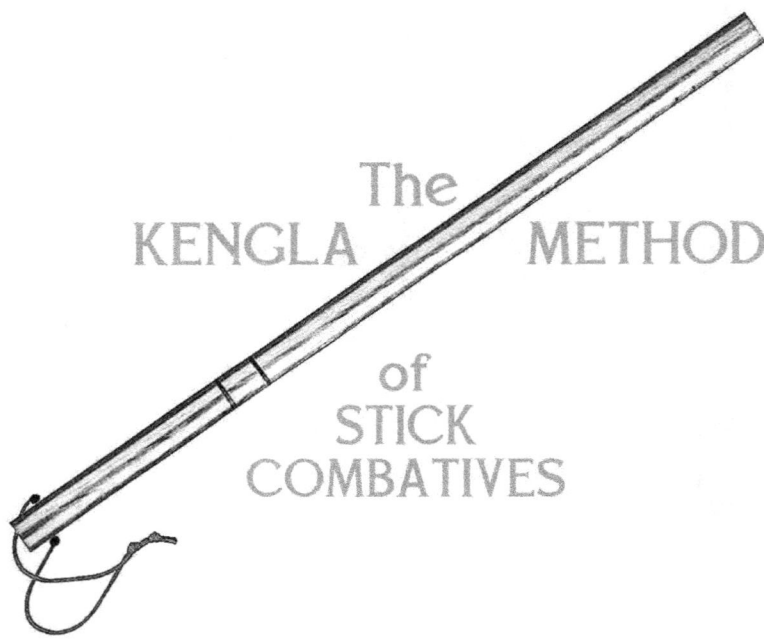

The
KENGLA METHOD
of
STICK
COMBATIVES

CHOKES AND GRAPPLING

The Death Triangle

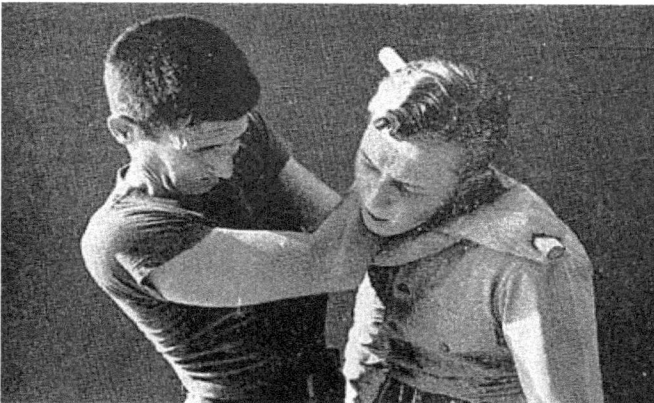

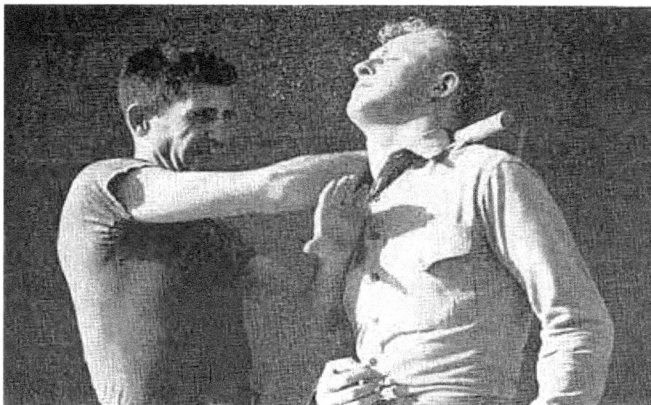

All right, you missed again. Your blow failed to drop your opponent. Don't worry, you are now in a position to back smash with your right elbow. Make a HOOK with your stick by a slight movement of the wrist; come back across, hooking your opponent's neck with the stick.

YOUR LEFT-HAND SHOOTS ACROSS IN FRONT OF YOUR OPPONENT, GRABBING THE LONG END OF THE STICK.

This is it, Mac, now you've got it made! Your opponent's neck is now uncomfortably nestled in the DEATH TRIANGLE. The stick behind his neck forms one side, your CROSSED arms on his throat are the other Two sides. SNAP THE TRIANGLE SHUT AND SQUEEZE!

The Reverse Death Triangle

Incidentally, this Triangle Treatment is excellent for curing enemy sentries who have "shouting sickness." You will find that it is a neat, silent way of dropping the sentry from behind. The triangle is simply reversed. To attack an enemy from the rear, form hook with the stick and your arm. Whip the stick across front of enemy's throat. Cross your right arm with your left and grasp the stick with your left hand. Then snap triangle shut and apply pressure. Squeeze until you feel his windpipe close; he can be revived! To kill, squeeze hard!

Police Escort Technique

When you "escort" an offender through a crowd, you may wish to move behind-him. To move him RAPIDLY and with VERY LITTLE resistance, grasp your stick in the middle; insert it, end first, between his legs and turn the whole stick so that it crosses his thighs; then move it UPWARDS. At the same time grasp the back of his collar with the free hand and PUSH FORWARD. In this manner you will be able to carry him along on his tip toes and completely off balance. This technique is very effective for quick, short trips from curb to wagon or from bar to street. The use of the stick as a horizontal bar is an excellent technique for the law enforcement officer.

He may take his stance in a relaxed manner, his stick horizontal, without conveying the obvious intention of a club raised in a striking pose. YET HE IS IN READINESS TO STRIKE instantly at the offender's hand, forearm, elbow, knee cap or shinbone. The advantage of this technique is the opponent's uncertainty about the direction from which the blow will come. The officer may release either hand and strike with the other. He will do this without premeditation, making his attack without any indication of the side from which it will come.

But whether you're a cop on a beat, a guy walking home from a date late at night, or a mud-sloshing' infantry man, if you're weaponless except for a "stick", these few tips will have given you something to rely on in case of an unforeseen attack. The stick is a versatile weapon and its technique rises far above the common thought of bashing in your opponent's head. And that's a good defense, too.

A PARTING THOUGHT

I have been tangentially involved with the Combatives Community since the mid-1980s, and throughout that involvement I have been fortunate to learn lessons that complemented the teachings of my original instructors. In that time, I have *also* had to sit through the diatribes of some Combatives exponents who, sadly, demonstrate that we're "not all cut from the same cloth."

Some Combatives practitioners were initially drawn to this field because they dislike the seeming "assembly line" structure of the Asian martial arts. Other practitioners do not mind the structure, but prefer the simplified effectiveness of these Combatives systems, which were originally designed to instill new recruits with practical combat-readiness in the short eight weeks they spent in Boot Camp. Still others are attracted to Combatives by the fact that the methods represent British and American derivatives of Eastern arts—a version more suited to our Western culture. All this is well and good ...

However, there exist in the last group a few toxic individuals who come to Combatives from a thinly-veiled racist perspective. Such practitioners can be heard to—

- deny the Asian influences found in Combatives
- boast of the superiority of Combatives to all Eastern arts
- attest that they refuse to learn anything at the hands of, as they often put it, "little *yellow* or *brown* men."

These are actual comments I have heard in my workshops and seminars; and it is disturbing to discover that such practitioners join our ranks in Combatives not because of its practical efficacy, but because they feel it bolsters their racist outlooks.

Of course, only *experience*—and not argument or discussion—can undo a person's racism. Thus, changing anyone's views is not my place nor my goal—but such practitioners should bear in mind that, in the same way that we all bleed red when cut, a focused chop to the throat will *crush* it, regardless of whether the person executing it calls it a *shuto*, a *knife-hand*, or an *edge-of-the-hand blow* ...

—James Loriega
Ninpokai Hombu

"I think what he's saying is that a Tanbo will crack a skull as quickly as a Military Stick."

Addenda

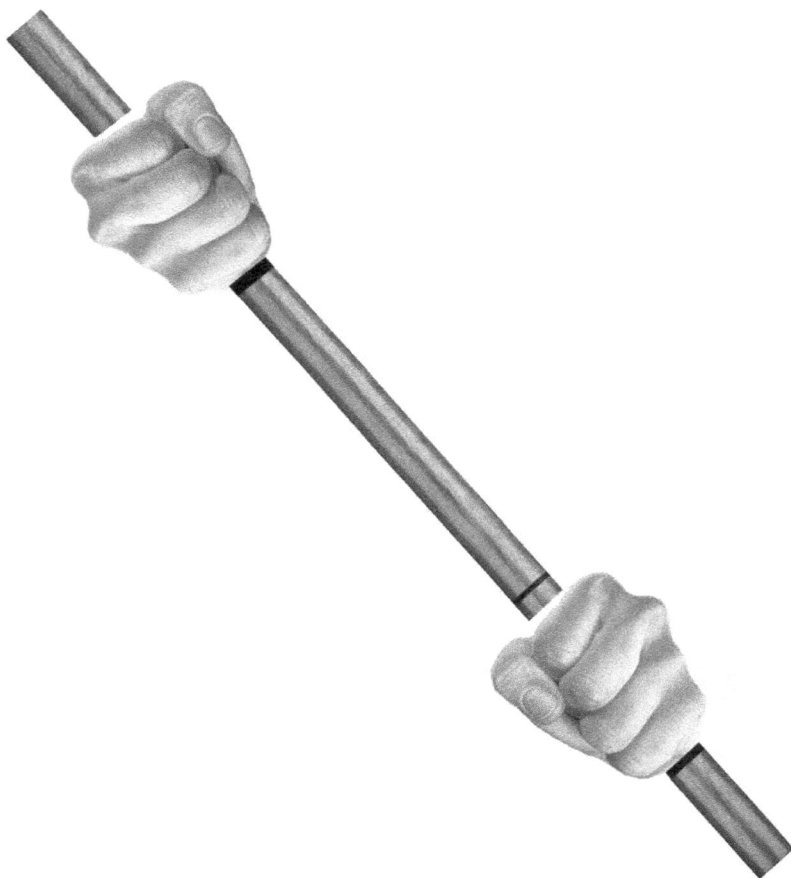

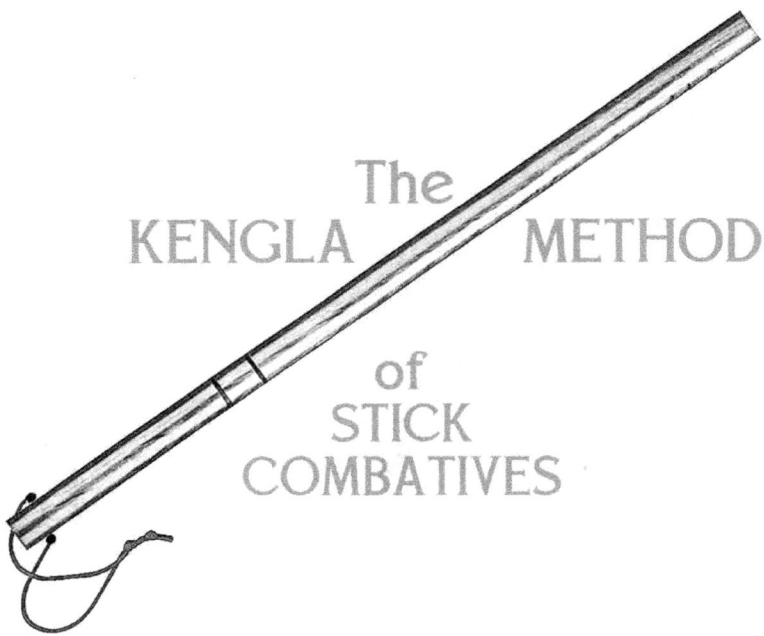

The
KENGLA METHOD
of
STICK
COMBATIVES

Safety In Training

Safety is the paramount consideration during any training activity. We train so that we can protect ourselves and not get hurt. Why then would we allow being hurt in training? It is the responsibility of the instructor and all class participants to ensure the safety of all. All participants in a training activity should be led through a proper warm up and stretching routine before class begins.

Safety Equipment

Practitioners should also use appropriate safety equipment for all training sessions. Equipment that should be used includes:

☒	*Athletic Cup*	☒	*Forearm Shields*
☒	*Athletic Mouth Piece*	☒	*Safety Goggles*
☒	*Safety Head Gear*	☒	*Safety Gloves*

Safety Training Weapons

Practitioners should also use safe training weapons. A variety of training blades should be used from rubber to aluminum trainers. Dulled Live blades are inappropriate for anything but solo training purposes.

No Live Weapons Should Ever Be Allowed In The Training Area.

Other Considerations

Training should be conducted in reasonable proximity of emergency medical care Training should be conducted in a designated training area with adequate flooring, padding, and ventilation.

Force Continuum

The force continuum is a conceptual tool which exists to aid person in determining what level of force is required and justified in controlling the actions of an assailant. Verbal commands, escort techniques, mechanical controls, and deadly force are all options which are available to a Practitioner depending upon the assailant's actions. Force escalation must cease when the assailant complies with the commands of the Practitioner, and/or the situation is controlled by the Practitioner. The model presented bellow consists of five levels. Physical defensive tactics are appropriate from levels three to five.

Level One: The assailant cooperates with the Practitioner's verbal commands. Physical actions are not required.

Level Two: The assailant is unresponsive to verbal commands. Assailant cooperation however is achieved with escort techniques.

Level Three: The assailant actively resists the Practitioner's attempts to control without being assault. Compliance and control holds, as well as pain compliance techniques are appropriate actions at this time.

Level Four: The assailant assaults a Practitioner or another person with actions which are likely to cause bodily harm. Appropriate action would include mechanical controls or defensive tactics such as stunning techniques. Impact and chemical weapons may be appropriate at this level.

Level Five: The assailant assaults a person or another person with actions which are likely to cause serious bodily harm or death if not stopped immediately. Appropriate actions would include deadly force through mechanical controls, impact weapons or firearms. Deadly force should be considered **only** when lesser means have been exhausted, are unavailable, or cannot be reasonably employed.

Decision of Force

When making the decision to use force a person should use the minimal amount of "reasonable" force necessary to safely control the situation at hand. When using deadly force for self-defense a person must be prepared to articulate and justify their use of a force.

Reasonable force can be defined as—

Force that is not excessive and is the least amount of force that will permit safe control of the situation while still maintaining a level of safety for himself or herself and the public.

A person is *justified* in the use of force when they reasonably believe it to be necessary to defend themselves or another from bodily harm and have no avenue for reasonable escape.

Escalation and de-escalation of resistance and response may occur without going through each successive level. The person has the option to escalate or disengage, repeat the technique, or escalate to any level at any time. However, the person will need to justify any response to resistance. If the person skips levels, he or she must explain why it was necessary to do so.

Totality of Circumstances

Totality of circumstances refers to all facts and circumstances known to the person at the time. The totality of circumstances includes consideration of the assailant's form of resistance, all reasonably perceived factors that may have an effect on the situation, and the response options available to the person.

Sample factors may include the following:

o   Severity of the assault or battery
o   Assailant is an immediate threat
o   Assailant's mental or psychiatric history, if known to the person
o   Assailant's violent history, if known to the person
o   Assailant's combative skills
o   Assailant's access to weapons
o   Innocent bystanders who could be harmed
o   Number of assailant's vs. number of persons
o   Duration of confrontation
o   Assailant's size, age, weight, and physical condition
o   The person's size, age, weight, physical condition, and defensive tactics expertise
o   Environmental factors, such as physical terrain, weather conditions, etc.

In all cases where your assessment and decision are questioned you may need to demonstrate the following:

o   That you felt physically threatened by and in danger from the suspect, i.e. that the suspect's behavior (body language/ words / actions) were aggressive and threatening;

o   That you used force as a last resort, and that you used the reasonable amount;

o   That you stopped using force once you had the suspect and the situation under control.

o   That the Practitioner has exhausted all reasonable efforts to escape the situation.

Sample Force Continuum

Subject Action	Practitioner Response
Cooperation	Verbal Commands
Passive Resistance	Escort Control
Active Resistance	Control & Compliance Holds
Assault Which Can Result in Bodily Harm	Defensive Tactics/Mechanical Controls/Less Lethal Weapons
Assault Which Can Result In Serious Bodily Harm or Death	Deadly Force

The use of **Force Continuum** presented is a general model based on common U.S. Use of Force guidelines. The continuum presented is for illustrative purposes only.

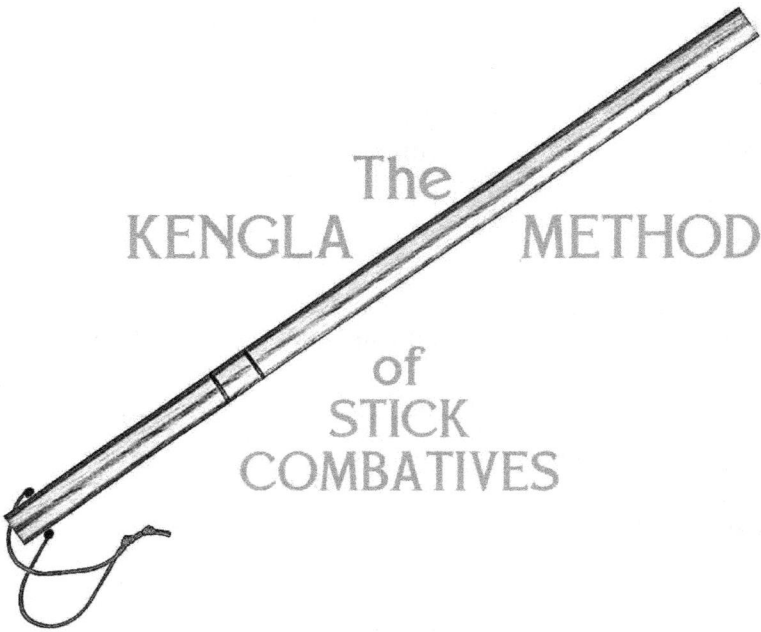

The
KENGLA METHOD
of
STICK
COMBATIVES

Conflict Anatomy

The basic study of human anatomy is essential to Defensive Tactics training. The information acquired is important in two respects. First individuals must be aware of the vulnerable points of the body in order to better protect themselves from assaults by others. Secondly, individuals must be conscience of what effects their counter measures and mechanical controls will have on a subject. Use of inappropriate force by an individual can quickly become a tragedy for all involved.

Points of the Human Body

When using stunning techniques, an individual must be mindful that there is no safe area on the body which to target. The effects of any stunning technique on a subjects body is nearly impossible to predict.

The study of *Conflict Anatomy* can give the individual only probable answers at best. An individual must consider the totality of circumstances when using stunning techniques. The amount of force necessary to be effective or in the inverse, use excessive force will depend on many factors.

Size is one easily identifiable factor. A smaller, physically less powerful individual may not expect the same effect of a stun that a large powerful individual might. The size of the subject must also be taken into consideration when evaluating which stunning techniques are most appropriate. The stunning targets and their effects presented here are a general guideline used for informative and illustrative purposes only. Ultimately an individual must abide by their agency's use of force policy, as well as any local state and federal laws which pertain to use of force before using physical force on a subject in either capacity as an individual or civilian.

Presented below are targets for stunning targets divided into three levels.

Level OneTargets

Level One represents targets on a subject's body which when affected are unlikely to cause serious or permanent injury to a subject. These targets should be viewed as a primary option. Level Two represents targets on a subject's body which when effected are likely to cause a higher level of temporary and/or permanent trauma than Level One targets.

Forearm	Buttocks	Back of Hand
Shoulder	Lower abdomen	Inside of wrist
Shoulder Blades	Upper Arm	Shin
Calf	Achilles tendon	Thigh
Instep		

Level Two Targets

A stun to a Level Two target has a higher risk for significant injury to a subject. A transition from a level one to a level two target should be considered by the individual when—

- A Level One target proves ineffective in controlling the subject
- A Level One target is inaccessible
- When a subject must be immediately controlled.

Knee Joint	Elbow Joint
Rib Cage	Collar Bone

Level Three Targets

Level Three targets are last resort lethal force targets. An individual should never attempt a stun to these targets unless the individual fears that the subject poses a threat of death or seriously injure to the individual or another.

Spine	Ear	Bridge of Nose	Eyes
Kidney	Throat	Lower Jaw	Tail Bone
Solar Plexus	Neck	Temple	Upper Jaw
Base of Neck	Groin		

Points of the Human Body, Front

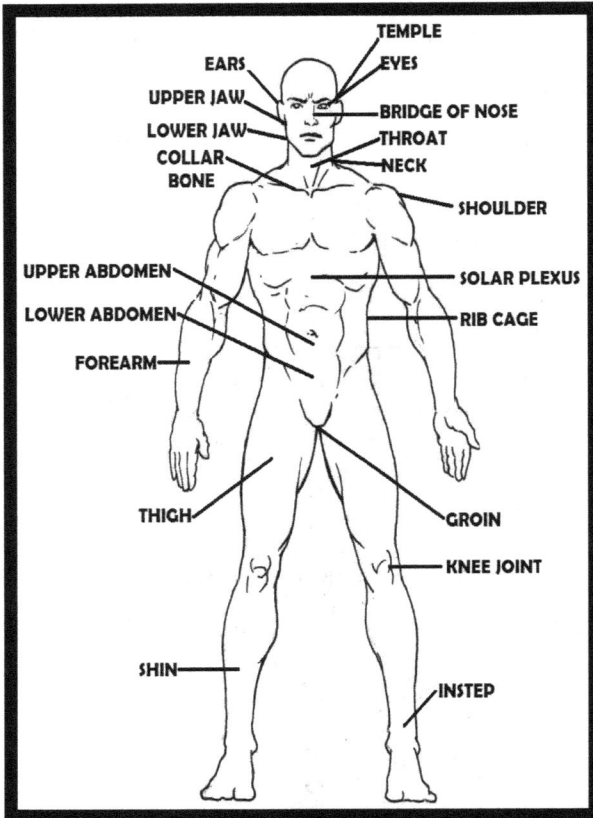

TEMPLE
EARS
EYES
UPPER JAW
BRIDGE OF NOSE
LOWER JAW
THROAT
COLLAR BONE
NECK
SHOULDER
UPPER ABDOMEN
SOLAR PLEXUS
LOWER ABDOMEN
RIB CAGE
FOREARM
THIGH
GROIN
KNEE JOINT
SHIN
INSTEP

Points of the Human Body, Rear

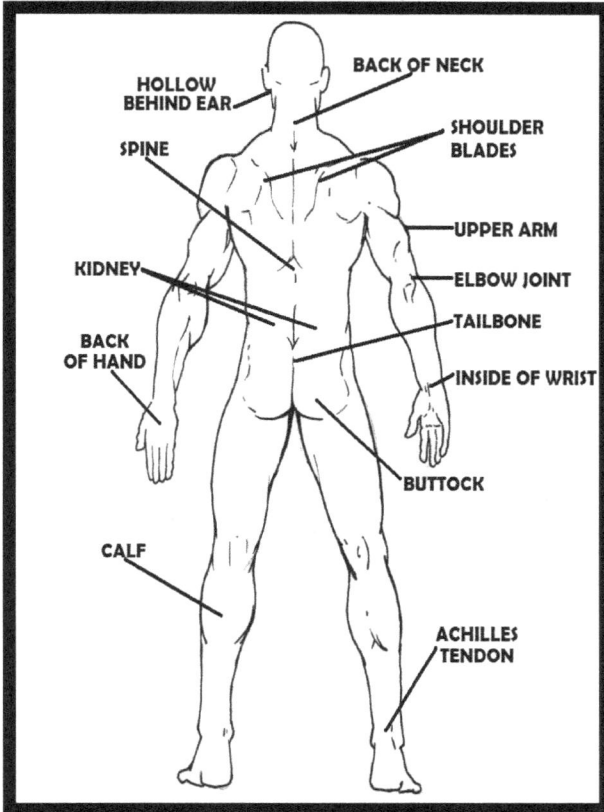

HOLLOW BEHIND EAR

BACK OF NECK

SPINE

SHOULDER BLADES

UPPER ARM

KIDNEY

ELBOW JOINT

TAILBONE

BACK OF HAND

INSIDE OF WRIST

BUTTOCK

CALF

ACHILLES TENDON

About
WILLIAM A. KENGLA
(6/25/1910 – 1/3/1993)

Col. William Archibald Kengla, USMC, was a highly-decorated Marine who was involved with some of the most significant military events of his time. William Kengla was born on June 25,1910, in Washington D.C.

Kengla served in the Naval Reserves and went on accept an appointment to the Naval Academy. He was commissioned in 1933 as a 2nd Lieutenat in the United States Marine Corps, and went on to attend the U.S. Army's *Chemical Warfare School*. Kengla served in the Virgin Islands, Tientsin, China, Iceland, and New Zealand as well.

Col. Wm. A. Kengla

Col Kengla was highly decorated and received several impressive recognitions during his career. For his service in Guadalcanal, Kengla was awarded the Silver Star Medal, the United States Armed Forces's third-highest personal decoration for valor in combat.The citation reads:

> *The President of the United States of America takes pleasure in presenting the Silver Star to Major William Archibald Kengla (MCSN: 0-4872), United States Marine Corps, for conspicuous gallantry and intrepidity as*

Commanding Officer of the 3rd Battalion, 6th Marines (Reinforced), 2nd Marine Division, in action against enemy Japanese forces on Guadalcanal, Solomon Islands, 19 January 1943.

When his battalion, attacking west along the Coast Road, suddenly encountered withering and demoralizing fire from concealed enemy forces, Maj Kengla, with inspiring leadership and utter disregard for his own personal safety, directed the extremely hazardous and laborious advance of his troops in the face of desperate hostile resistance. Dislodging the Japanese from their strong positions in the heavily camouflaged, narrow caves which had been dug into the sides of steep cliffs and ravines to serve as gun emplacements, his command was responsible for the complete destruction or forced retreat of the enemy.

Maj. Kengla's heroic conduct and valiant devotion to duty throughout the entire engagement contributed greatly to the success of this vital mission and were in keeping with the highest traditions of the United States Naval Service.

Kengla was awarded the ***Citation of Military Merit*** by the Korean Government for his service as President Syngman Rhee's senior military advisor. Similarly, the Netherlands awarded Col. Kengla the ***Order of the Orange-Nassau*** for his work in assisting the Netherlands Marine Corp in their preparations for the Java Campaign.

With respect to his background in personal combat, Kengla was a student of armed and unarmed combatives under A. J. Drexel Biddle, author of the now-classic military combatives manual, **Do or Die**. Kengla, in fact, contributed many of the attack and defense sequences found in the manual.

Kengla also contributed significantly to another classic manual, **Cold Steel**, written by John Styers, who was himself a student of Biddle. In his book, Stylers credits Kengla with the short stick method presented. (*Below right, Kengla's Silver Star medal*)

Kengla continued to make significant contributions even after leaving active service. In 1958, Kengla accepted a position as a Professor of Naval Science at the University of Texas at Austin. While there, he also served as the First Marine Commanding Officer of the NROTC unit, and later served as Director of the Austin-Travis County Civil Defense force until 1970. The highly decorated and accomplished Col. Kengla passed away on January 3rd 1993 in Austin Texas.

FERNAN VARGAS

Mr. Vargas is a lifelong martial artist who currently holds a Menkyo Kaiden in Bushi Satori Ryu as well as black belts and instructor rankings in Kuntao, Silat, Kuntaw, Jujutsu and Hapkido. As a certified Law Enforcement Defensive Tactics Instructor, Mr. Vargas has taught defensive tactics to law enforcement officers at the local, state, and federal level, as well as security officers, military personnel and private citizens from around the United States and foreign nations such as Canada, Italy, and Spain.

Mr. Vargas has developed programs which have been approved by the Police officer training and Standards Board of several states, and adopted by agencies such as the Pentagon Force protection Agency. Additionally, organizations such as the Fraternal Order of Law Enforcement and the International Academy of Executive Protection Agents have given formal endorsements of the programs developed by Mr. Vargas and Raven Tactical International. Mr. Vargas has been an instructor at the prestigious International Law Enforcement Educators & Trainers Association International Conference (ILEETA). Mr. Vargas currently holds instructor credentials in over 20 defensive tactics and combatives curriculums.

As an author Mr. Vargas has published several books on topics such as Law Enforcement Defensive Tactics, Knife Combatives, the Tomahawk, Native American Fighting Traditions, Crime Survival, and more. His writings have also appeared in numerous Industry periodicals.

www.TheRavenTribe.com
www.RavenTactical.com
www.RavenTalkPodcast.com
www.MartialBooks.com

JAMES LORIEGA

In 1984, James Loriega founded the **New York Ninpokai**, a training facility which soon came to be regarded as *"the premier academy for the traditional shinobi arts in NYC."* Loriega began his formal martial arts training in 1967 with the late Grandmaster Ronald Duncan, the first non-Japanese to teach the shinobi arts in the United States—and the acknowledged *Father of American Ninjutsu.* Though he later trained with other ninjutsu masters, it was from Duncan-sensei that Loriega learned the myriad strategies, tactics, techniques, and disciplines of the ancient *shinobi.*

In the mid- to late-80s, Loriega also trained in other martial arts, including *Aikijujutsu, Taijutsu, Jojutsu, and Hojojutsu.* He began writing extensively around that same time, and from 1985 to 1995 served as Technical Consultant and Contributing Editor for **Ninja** magazine, an international publication dedicated exclusively to ninjutsu.

In January of 2002, Loriega was recognized as a master in western arts by the ***International Masters-at-Arms Federation*** (IMAF), based in Milan, Italy. The IMAF, now dissolved, was an organization of professional instructors of Historical and Classical edged weapons.

In February of 2018, he was recognized by the ***Martial Arts University*** as a *Martial Arts Icon*—an individual who is symbolic of an idea and leaves a memorable mark on the lives of those he teaches.

In April of 2018, he was recognized as a *Ninjutsu Scholar* and inducted into the ***International Circle of Masters*** (ICM).

In November of 2019, inducted into the Grandmaters Hall of Fame by Soke Michael DePasquale, President of the **Martial Arts University**.

He has published over two dozen books on martial arts and martial culture, and his extensive writings have appeared in mainstream martial arts publications such as **Black Belt**, **Inside Kung-Fu**, **Ninja**, and **Tactical Knives**.

BIBLIOGRAPHY

Draeger, Donn F. **Asian Fighting Arts**. Tokyo, New York, San Francisco: Kodansha International, Ltd. 1969

Drexel Biddle, A. J. **Do or Die**: A Supplementary Manual on Individual Combat. Boulder, CO: Paladin Press. 1937

Fairbairn, William E. **Get Tough.** Boulder, CO: Paladin Press.

– **Scientific Self-Defense**. London: D. Appleton and Co. 1931

FitzMaurice, Eugene. **The Hawkeland Cache**. New York: Simon & Schuster. 1980

Gracián, Baltasar. **The Art of Worldly Wisdom**. Christopher Maurer, Trans. New York: Doubleday. 1991

Loriega, James. **The Urban Edge**: *Sharp Tactics for Street Survival*. New York: Pay-Per-Cut Press. 2017

– **Ghost Writing**: *The Tactical Pen in Personal Protection*. Washington, DC: Raven Tradecraft Press. 2018

– **Know Your Enemy**: *Conducting Opponent Research*. Washington, DC: Raven Tradecraft Press. 2018

– **The OSS Combat Manual**. Washington, DC: Raven Tradecraft Press. 2019

– **Dressed To Kill**. Washington, DC: Raven Tradecraft Press. 2019

Melton, H. Keith. **OSS Special Weapons and Equipment.** New York: Stirling Publishing Co., Inc. 1991

Smythe, M. (Col.) **When The Going Gets Tough**. Thousand Oaks, CA: Dragon Publishing Corp.1985

Styers, John. **Cold Steel**: *Technique of Close Combat*. Boulder, CO: Paladin Press. 1952

Vargas, Fernan D. **The Knife-Fighting of *Cold Steel***. Chicago, IL: Raven International. 2017

– **War Hawk Tomahawk**, Vol I – II. Chicago, IL: Raven International. 2017

– **Raven Tactical Self-Defense 101**. Chicago, IL: Raven International. 2018

– **Combat Machete. Chicago, IL:** Raven International. 2019

Other Titles by these Authors

- **Kukri** *Combat Knife of Nepal* Vol. I
- **Kukri** *Combat Knife of Nepal* Vol. II
- **Cuchillo Corvo:** *Combat Knife of Chile*
- **Knuckle Duster**: *A Guide to Using Brass Knuckles*
- **American Combat Masters**
- **Masters of the Blade**
- **Cane & Able** *Cane Combatives*

These Books and More, Available Now at

www.RavenTactical.com

www.ingramcontent.com/pod-product-compliance
Lightning Source LLC
Chambersburg PA
CBHW031605040426
42452CB00006B/412